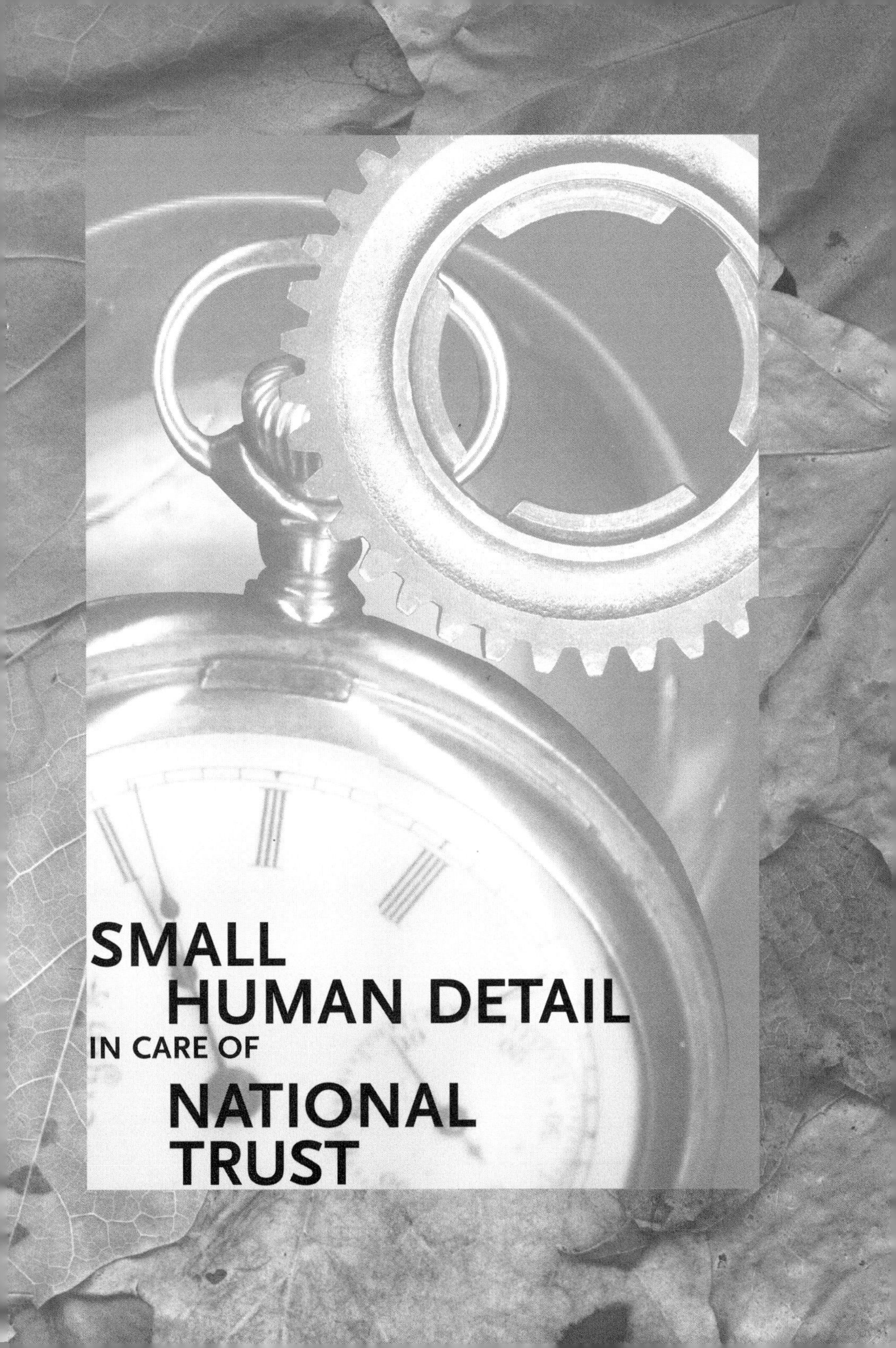

SMALL HUMAN DETAIL IN CARE OF NATIONAL TRUST

The New Issues Press Poetry Series

The New Issues Press Poetry Series is sponsored by The College of Arts and Sciences, Western Michigan University, Kalamazoo, Michigan

Printed in the United States of America.

First Edition, 2000.

ISBN: 0-932826-85-7 (paperbound)

Library of Congress Cataloging-in-Publication Data:
Walls, Martin
Small Human Detail in Care of National Trust/ Martin Walls
Library of Congress Catalog Card Number (99-076765)

Art Direction:	Tricia Hennessy
Design:	Ralph Stocker
Production:	Paul Sizer The Design Center, Department of Art College of Fine Arts Western Michigan University
Printing:	Courier Corporation

SMALL HUMAN DETAIL IN CARE OF NATIONAL TRUST

MARTIN WALLS

New Issues Press

WESTERN MICHIGAN UNIVERSITY

For my family & friends.
For Christine.

"Je ne puis rien dire, écrire (ni penser)
d'autre que ce que saison m'inspire."
—Francis Ponge Nioque de l'Avant Printemps

Contents

Part One

Part Two

Acknowledgments

The following poems, some in slightly different form, have been previously published:

32 Pages: "Small Human Detail in Care of National Trust"

Acts of Reading: A Literary and Cultural Studies Reader: "Socialist Poem #1"

American Literary Review: "Germinal"

Black Warrior Review: "Socialist Poem #3"

Boulevard: "Wrecking Yard"

The Community Times (Lafayette, IN): "Socialist Poem #1," "Socialist Poem #4"

Crazyhorse: "The Badger," "Train Wreck with Suicide"

Five Points: "Poem for the Magnolias"

The Gettysburg Review: "Meccano #2 Set"

Mankato Poetry Review: "Variation on 'Continuity' by Yannis Ritsos"

The Nation: "Knowledge of the End of Autumn"

Notre Dame Review: "Beneath Our World There's Nothing but Other Worlds"

The Ohio Review: "A Pornographer Considers His Garden"

Passages North: "Homage to César Vallejo"

Poem: "Late January"

Poetry Daily (www.poems.com): "Poem for the Magnolias"

Spoon River Poetry Review: "Tippecanoe River", "Dusk, Scircleville"

Part One

Knowledge of the End of Autumn

I am already familiar with the abysmal stupidity of insects
—J. Henri Fabre

Trees creak like old joists, & cold dismantles me beam by beam.
Leaves fall the way paint peels, until everything's primed
silver-gray.

On the porch opposite carpenters are swinging planks
from pulley lines.
Their nails go in *like that, like that*: so easy, from a gun.

You'd expect from them rollicking humor, beer cans
lobbed from a cooler,
But no, they're studied & sure: one measures, measures, cuts.
Another hoists a two-by-four quick as my hand to shade
My brow, to see exactly how they do it,

Dancing over the scaffold in black coveralls, like the paper
wasps that settled in a corner of my deck,
Framing their oak-gray fist-sized nest, filling a few sluggish cells.

What were they thinking? Last week the first frost chiseled in.
Since then, autumn's unhinging wind.

Yesterday, I saw the last of them drop from the nest.
With its blunt black head & wire-thin thorax it was a loosened nail;
With legs, winding slowly down; an abdomen, arching sweetly two
or three times.
Life's simple mechanism.

Then how do we act?

After Reading *The Queen of the Air* by John Ruskin

Cloth stretched over the walnut skeleton of an antique chair.
Lazy brownian motion of horsehair dust in blades of sunlight.

Upholstery tools: a crescent-shaped sailor's needle, cloth shears,
  a hilt of ash on the screwdriver.
Pliers & pincers lying about like heavy artillery.

Father guides my fingers. Three tacks go in & out his mouth,
  like organ stops.
His words make quick runs: "let the *tools* guide you, son."

I'm holding his father's hammer, smooth as a femur, insistent
  as blood.
I tap firmly, trying to wake the dead:

My grandfather, Albert, who built Pullman cars in Brighton
  between the wars,
Until dust & ashes filled his lungs with froth—

I've seen his cars at the steam museum; temples of craft, of an
  occult religion;
In them, in the cuneiform of work, I've glimpsed that other world

Of hand-carved mahogany window frames; of dense satin weave
  on seat covers;
The sweet-heavy machine-music of brass switches & steel handles;

Every chassis-rivet hand-peened; each
Perfect pit holding its own spit of light—

If only I could make this hammer do the will of my hand
The way my pen unravels its yards & yards of guilt.

Brighton Fish Market

1.
The flounder: cubist fish: four-dimensional idea in two-dimensions;
Both eyes screwed atop its rolled-out face contemplate sin,

While monkfish offer up their ascetic flesh.

2.
Skates shuffled in a shallow tray, a deck of wet cards.
Red & black spots on their slick backs; the ones on top, clubs
& diamonds,
A good hand in cribbage—

But, wait, those are blow flies!
Tiny self-propelled shuttles of smell & sound.

3.
Dab, sprats, hake, cod, rock salmon: their eyes are secret windows
Behind which one imagines an industry of surveillance.

Filleted, their bones become old fashioned television antennae.

4.
The crab basket's a mass grave of ribs, femurs, ilia, flattened skulls.
The rattling skeletons of drowned sailors. There is no escape.

Though, once, in St. Valéry-en-Caux, I saw one scramble
Dans un panier sans que Madame ou Monsieur-le-Poissonier
ne les voient.

5.
Whelks, winkles, cockles, mussels: stones that dreamed of life
& woke to find themselves halfway there.

6.
After sundown fishing skiffs congregate beyond the marina.
You can just make out their winking lamps like watches slipped
    in & out of waistcoats.

All night, the taut lines dip in a waxy sea,
While plaice wait on the sea floor, remote & vengeful gods.

7.
Whiting, herring, mackerel, huss: dark's roe swells in their bellies;
Night's tar-black tide spills into the market—

There goes a swirled mulch of sawdust & blood; string-tied
    bundles of day-old news.
Someone flicks on a bulb-constellation.

8.
In the plaice tray one fillet remains.
It is a fat, translucent moon, exactly poised between solid & wet.

Touch it & your hand will go through to the next life.

Exile

How does one show contrition to a city?
Or reassemble a flotsam of memory untouched by exile's
tide-slow erasure?

And who can say with confidence, three thousand miles away,
that something other than nostalgia
Explains this ardor for the commonplace?

For the burnt crust of close-packed houses atop those hills;
the soot-black trees in the salt-soaked air.
The sky the color of bleached bone, or a cleaned fish; white
as knuckles gripping the beach-rail hard.
For the hush of backwashing waves; barnacles closing callused
eyes; seaweed clutching wet fists of stone.

For fishing boats chained above the storm beach; the sea's
mixture of milk & glass,
From which, in summer, divers would emerge, pulling their face-
gear off as if Brighton were a new world, safe to breathe.

They'd lay their gifts on the table: rusted buckles, frosted bottles,
crusted coins, oil cans, playing cards,
A bottled message, calling with its distant voice: *If you find this,
please return my note—*

The door of the sea had cracked open—

Primer

Clotted heat. The brush mats & paint gums the ferrule.
I sit back, exhausted. Then reach for thinners.

All day like this, priming a railing fence, sweat stinging my eyes,
The iron too hot to grip & endless as summer.

On the sidewalk water guns & hoses make dappled pools;
Cardinals & robins squat breast-bone deep; the grass
combed in ecstatic swirls.

Cricket-squirt & bird-shrill. The lawn sprinkler metronomes,
And the songs of high-pitched girls tumble like church bells—

This is the music of childhood's inner country, its geography
I know by heart:
The quick tug of bandaids; the smell of witch-hazel & camphor;
lemonade's sickly quench—

Now the maple shadows are stretched like bodies in a dream,
And I see my shadow is crowned with light reflecting
from windows behind me.

I stand, stripped to the waist.
My hog-bristle brush is a flag in my hand, & when I move
the crown of light moves.

Socialist Poem #1

England: "The Winter of Discontent," 1978-79

I am seven & see things simply, as a fish does. I can see the flat colors of the 1970s: greens, browns, cold grays like fading Kodachrome. I see the unburied of the gravedigger's strike, the bat-black mortuaries crawling with terror. And monsterish heaps of uncollected trash bags, evil smelling, pulling snow into their black folds as if they're pantomime villains making off with the hero.

All day scavenging seagulls squark in a festering sky. Evenings, the sounds of crisis mix with the smell of frying fat, pungent Polish coal. On TV, I watch Mr. Callaghan sing "I'm the Man Who Waters the Workers' Beer" at the Labour Party conference. Later, he's beetling from Number 10 in his shiny black Bentley.

Socialists. Their winter's as cold & harsh as nylon sheets. At six thirty electricity's cut off, the union on a three day week. So we sit in the kitchen while mum smokes her thin cigarettes & grandma's reminded of the war. Hazy blue light from the gas stove throws crazy shadows against the wall; doom-dark drifts against the house, an awful reverse snow. Above the rattle of boiling spuds my transistor radio speaks a strange tongue: *tripartite bargaining, arbitration*, it trills.

Seven o'clock: soon dad'll be home, hair slick from snow-drizzle, no shower till the heater growls awake. Nine thirty: I fold icy sheets around me, keeping the curtains open. The moon glows like a pilot light. All winter, I've watched filaments of ice lay down shapes in the corner of the window: a spaceship, a fabulous continent, a rose. Tonight, a hand sets out. It grows into one of grandpa's big, bony hands. Only it grows bigger than that, more scary. Pane after pane in its clutch.

Homage to César Vallejo

The architects of Spring have erected an immense & spangled vault.
The weather & the land lie beneath it, locked in furious passion.
We should be warned, for, in the nonhuman, survival precedes
Even touch, or breath, or love: the silver maple's redundant with seeds

Before its leaves have stretched their bloody fingers, & cherry trees
Look clumsy in their blossoms, wearing the clothes we threw in haste,
Because today, without speaking, we decided on chance.

Strange, serious weather. Her eyes brewed storm cells on an afternoon
When the rain's crystal net made the world heavy as a sigh.
I was defenseless; a cornfield bruised by pools of blue-silver water,
Her tongue touching down tornado after tornado,

While cloud-hands roamed the parched country until the secret cities
Of my skin prayed for relief. A song welled in her breasts;
Putting my lips to them, I became a choir of praise to benevolent gods.

And, from that defiance, when I rose & stepped through the door,
Two sparrows entered my life & built their nest.

“A God not of *forces* but *things*.”

Snail inches to the edge of morning & lifts its head,
    a semi-liquid question mark.
April. Maple buds channel raindrops through their gargoyle shapes.
Light drips from a roof of branches.

Half the vinca laid in—

If growth is the analogy of faith, then this kneeling's prayer,
And the simple act of gardening grounds a theology
    of the particular,

Where pillbugs are angels, & cicadas, white as saints,
    curl in the paradisiacal clay.
Moths ascend the mortal world on wings torn from a Bible—

And what else is flitting & worming, in the mulch of memory?
Something a priest once said, in private, about “a personal God.”

Something his brethren would never buy.

Cicadas at the End of Summer

Whine as though a pine tree is bowing a broken violin;
As though a bandsaw cleaves a thousand thin sheets of titanium;
They chime like freight wheels on a Norfolk Southern slowing
    into town.

But all you ever see is the silence.
Husks, glued to the underside of maple leaves.
With their nineteen fifties Bakelite lines they'd do just as well
    hanging from the ceiling of a space museum—

What cicadas leave behind is a kind of crystallized memory;
The stubborn detail of, the shape around a life turned

The color of forgotten things: a cold broth of tea & milk
    in the bottom of a mug,
Or skin on an old tin of varnish you have to lift with lineman's pliers.
A fly paper that hung thirty years in Bird Cooper's pantry in Brighton.

Socialist Poem #2

April 1976. A month before the General Election & this is Socialism. I stand in a basement flat among a bric-a-brac of pipes & cigarettes, pale ale & tea cups, Battenburg cake. A red rosette has been pinned above my heart: *VOTE GEORGE*, it says. Harry George, that is, in tweed; his face bright, but peaked, like the last of spring's chatty narcissus. With him is my father, & others, like thanes around a Saxon king.

We are in Brighton Kemptown constituency, where I'd quick-foot behind my parents on weekends to canvass the council estates: Whitehawk, Falmer, Moulscoombe. These are hard places, even for the South. Hove is different: our houses are made of brick & flint & pebble-dash; no cement terraces there, dull as welfare dentures. And we have streets lined with chestnuts & sycamores that live long enough for cancer's burned sugar to bubble on their bark. And it's safe: me & Charles & Nicholas running around half the night, our neighbors edgy as blue hydrangea with our laughter & screams.

The council estate kids were wild. We'd spit out their hard names (Carl & Gary & Dean) in defense, defenseless. They were the truants & troublemakers; later, when news seeped through as if from trenches, the petty thieves, addicts, suicides. Sometimes the old anger returns, as fast & useless as my punches. But sometimes I forgive them: Jack Dineen, the soccer captain (that brilliant thug), who kicked me off the first eleven; how does he live, I wonder, his professional career in ruins?

It is May, the Sunday before election day, & my father is young, crazily mustached. Falmer is torched by a fantastic sunset. Carl & Gary & Dean are, I imagine, in church, suited & brushed.

Now here come those old sodium lamps humming on with their what's-new gossip. And there goes a town fox, nosing the boozy air, & a pipistrelle sweeping by eraser-easy. Then that deep cerulean fills the sky as when, in chemistry, the teacher would pour blue vitriol safely behind his screen.

November, the Wabash River

The Electrolux is covered with leaves—what's it doing so far
from houses?
It's a dead animal in the snow, the dust sack shrunk around
its iron rib.

Aspens shake their plasticky leaves at me, & kids
Have snapped yarrow stalks like aerials until they stop tuning in
the other side.

Don't worry: final communiqués have been written on what's
discarded here:
"Cricket!" says a dead lighter, "Sunny Delight!" a plastic juice
bottle, "This Bud's For You."

Walking home, chlorine drums bear the skulls of those who
dreamed of a better future
And were buried in that dream—

We are the earth's.

For the Roses

We're dismissed to the rose garden before flames are lit; a new
 gaggle
Of somber-driven cars already slaloming our bedraggled group.

A purple plume-shadow snakes across the lot.
I look up: steel smoke-stack, rook-black smoke, & blue sky
 opened like another card: *Our sympathies for your loss—*

Because there's no chance for a proper grave now
 the cemeteries are filled,
Room for no more, because Brighton's spread like bindweed
 from sea to hill.

Downtown, an old church yard's ploughed under to make way
 for Eagle Life Insurance.
I watched the stark yellow backhoes eating the gruesome earth;
Saw the salt-washed tombstones stacked against the wall,
 souls turned under like mulch.

Now there's this crematorium at the crest of Bear Road;
The last—no kidding—building in town.

We're up here more & more these days;
My great-aunts—Chum, Joan, Doris—meeting among the
 memorial roses as if death were just a cribbage drive.
But mother's telling me about one before them,
 her grandmother. Her roses.

The secret was horseshit.
She'd follow brewery wagons around Ditchling village
 with a sugar sack & coal scoop,
Clip-clopping in her hob-nails, her skirts unfurling in the breeze.

"It's for the roses," she'd call out to friends & clergy, her shovel
poised.
When she died they pressed her body in the ground like a cutting.

"Hide this," mother says, & hands me a stem.
Later, it'll be growing like a morning's worth of light on the kitchen
sill.

My mother loves white roses the most, the ones with the varicose
petals.
When she kneels to ash their roots she reminds me of her own
veins, ridged & swollen when she birthed me.

Mother & our neighbors tend their roses like children.
They coo to them in baby talk: *Rosey is bootiful, bootiful rosey.*
They're always trying new feeding techniques, or new cures
for the canker spots & rust.

Last spring some guys came round the neighborhood, selling
sweet-smelling ash out of a van, a fiver a bag.
It was for the roses, they said. It was better than fishmeal,
or woodchips, or peat moss.

It brought the roses back from the dead; it burst open their colors:
The red splash of rainclouds at dawn, or a sun-shocked field
of yellow straw.

They put out bud after thumb-fat bud—

So it was a shame when those guys were arrested.
It was human ash, see. From Bear Road crematorium.
Such a pity, because the roses never looked better;
professional, almost,

Like these in the memorial garden, with their flesh-thick leaves
    & stems straight as spines.
Their flush heads nodding.

X-Ray

While looking for a fracture, a single black hair, the doctor says
    my toe bones are *beautiful*.
My phalanges lined neat & small, the ivory keys of a child's piano,

And someone's ploughed dark furrows between the metatarsi:
Bones white as moonlight on steel, white as frozen snow-strips
    on the riffled soil.

Wrecking Yard

after A.R. Ammons "Motion for Motion."

Midwinter. An oilstone sky. The river's diesel-slow freight of ice.
The moon sharpens its chisel edge.
        Clouds close in.

Taillights' swollen eyes blink through a stream of steaming exhaust,
Then narrow to a distant admonition: *please don't.*
        We humans.

Indiana winter grinds its transmission, opens its throttle;
Snow-eddies pinion to rectilinear icicles
        On bridge struts—

And if there is *automatic machinery in things*,
Is there not, reciprocating, life,
        No less ingenious?—

The wrecking yard: Fords, Plymouths, GM trucks on blocks; frost-bitten
Rust-fingers on fenders; a snow-shagged shrub punching
        The grille of a Chevy.

And, in me, memory produces its own nuclear force. My father,
Half-kidding, saying my Renault was alive.
        Saying "Talk to it . . ."

In the snow-buzz of atoms
        Worlds geared within worlds.

Variation on "Continuity" by Yannis Ritsos

We too know the soil well
(Or know the soil too well), how it fights, refuses:
Spuds, beans, marrow, scrawny tomato,
    but sometimes figs or bitter grapes,
And, higher each year, stones are piled
Like tiny cairns neatly next to rows.

While digging a trench Father strikes a tree root.
He feels the ancient jolt go up the pick handle
Into his raw shoulder & cries *Jesus*.
I look up from the spade, & see the apple tree,
And know its old, gray twist to be bones
    aching in my father's back.

The Cold War in England

1.
It was History, & we were bored with the bald facts of Black
Plague, when, suddenly, a motorbike revved-up outside;
The first note of its motor climbing through dead leaves exactly
like an air-raid siren.

Heads turned. Even unflappable Mr. Charles', his chalk paused
mid-cursive, as that second split open, raw with fear,
Until the easy clutch brought back the mid-morning music:
a slick-running motor, fluorescent hum, the chalk's sweet
monotonous click.

2.
I remember one night in particular: a Scouts meeting
at Cardinal Newman School in Hove,
The broad summer sky lit by rail sparks from the London-
Brighton line, & me
Actually thinking it was the end of the world; that it would look
like this, terrible, beautiful—

I was too busy with death to play red rover in the dusk-blue
field, dew climbing the grass like mayflies;
Too scared to sleep whenever the hills trapped a sea-storm
& settled its slow barrage above the town;

And every jet that flew by, gear down for Gatwick, held
the bomb to its belly like a rugger ball.
I really was a morbid kid.

3.
Soon as it arrived I pinned up the map of nuclear targets.
U.S. bases mostly: East Anglia was splashed with huge red-
shaded loci that showed the blast size.

I put my hand over the bulbous bit & imagined England
with its backside blown clean off.
Elsewhere, there were safe, pale-green spaces, mainly the North
where survivors would live years underground.
Out of cans. Going root-mad.

The map was annotated.
Brighton, it said, was a *tertiary* target, having a *small* power
station, being the *possible* seat of *makeshift* government.

Which was like saying our soccer team was *only* in the *second*
division, &—I admit—this was disappointing;
Our blood-red detonation no bigger than a half-penny.

Tippecanoe River

For Christine

A heron's neck smokes through a cross-hatch of cottonwoods.
An inch above the surface firecracker flies explode.
A breeze combs the maples, light tumbles out like hair.
The water eddies & dimples.

When you lean in a paddle, the river consents & gives us
    motion, direction, sends us crazily bank to bank.
Damselflies cruising beside us on wings salvaged from
    the skeletons of willow leaves.
Hawks dip & rise above, loving the air, the way it presses
    against them.

Raccoon tracks & deer tracks. A muskrat chases us, then dips
    into a cornfield.
A sudden cry of heat, & a white bass snaps its body the way
    you do your fingers
When you remember something funny, or beautiful—

I want to imitate all the ways the world says it loves you;
The way a kingfisher plunges beneath the water, an ingot
    of pure silver;
The cobwebs that clutch & hold the light.

Small Human Detail in Care of National Trust

1.
The guide said much about the house: how it was built, fortified,
 how it declined.
How room after squat room closed until the caretaker died
 in 1969, Lord of Wet Rot & three decrepit towers.
The fourth—I found it—lost in laburnum & bulrush.

But nothing of small human detail: the deeply cupped stone steps
 leading down to the moat,
The name etched on a window behind the stairwell curtain:
 Eliz. Thomas 1712,
Next to it four diamonds carved in the shape of one.

2.
Sandstone cliffs above the house, & view of the Downs: arable
 fields, copses, two farmhouses, affable sheep, a windmill.
Father handed me his strange camera, foregrounding himself
 with mother, arm in arm.

It was one of those old-fashioned jobs that opens like a magic box,
 capturing the world on its ground-glass screen.
One you huddle over, holding it the way a surgeon might cup
 a replacement heart.
I turned the chrome handle & let it spring back. The click was
 enormous.

3.
But I have no skill. I had shrub leaves in focus at the frame's edge,
 & the center, my parents, all cloud.
Should've been watching a diamond in the middle of the screen
 shift from black to blank & back.
I should've brought the image & its ghost-image together.

But for all my fiddling—0.8 to infinity—my parents & their pale-
    yellow doubles refused each other.
In the smudged print you can see father's furious waving,
    & my mother, there, mouthing something I didn't hear.

Ightam Mote, England

A Pornographer Considers His Garden

Hot. The lawn's glassy, shrubs un-focused, as if someone
Smeared the lens with Vaseline.

These could be a series of medium shots from a stud movie:
A beetle switching by in Metrocolor;
Oregano bushy & fertile-looking as private hair.

A slug rolls back its hood.
I zoom in.

A bee thrums at the pinkish sex of a columbine,
And tiny weevils carry their length prouder
Than any actor.

Now I know what's beautiful was meant to be hidden from sight.
Flashes of it now & then.

What inspiration—!
I *flirt* with the world.

Part Two

Poem for the Magnolias

Magnolias are opening their raw & awkward hearts as if they are
about to confess to a perfect crime.

Before the magnolia flowers, it was the time of fat, bruised
buds; all the cats in Hove Park Road were unapproachable.

It's raining. I'm late for work, frustrated. I must be more like
the magnolia!

The way their petals swell all-at-once, then over-extend,
over-excited for life.

Is it the curve on magnolia petals that makes the notes of ring
doves so round, or vice versa?

Everyday, on my way to the wine store, I see the magnolias;
pleasure more exquisite than my tea-break, or stealing
a pack of Marlboro.

A magnolia blooms. The sea is calmed. Fish throw themselves
onto hooks.

When a magnolia flower unfurls it lets go a cry inaudible
to humans.

There should be wine made from magnolia petals, to be drunk
chilled with quail's eggs & salmon, or duck à la pêche with
waterchestnuts.

The rain-smudged bark of the magnolia, the flowers scattered
like lit windows in a dark street.

Today, both the sun & moon try to imitate a magnolia flower.

Now the magnolias have blossomed summer can continue. Dr. Dossiter may go on vacation, Mr. White can quit worrying about his tomatoes.

A magnolia flower opens in the middle of the evening: electricity flickers on & off.

On my way to work I remember to take in the magnolias. That evening I'm £5 up on my till.

Steel-black woodlice on a magnolia branch, & the roseate moonlight shining on them!

Magnolia petals say *white*, but they mean *pink*.

The *Botanical History of Sussex* by Gerald Legg does not include the cultivation of magnolias, which do not mind, confident of their influence.

I hear laughter coming from the magnolias.

A magnolia flower awakens, takes stock of its whereabouts, careful not to speak too harshly.

These four trees have bloomed together, democratically. When they vote, they all vote for the Magnolia Party.

A magnolia bud! Its aperture of petals unwinding.

The petals of a magnolia flower are simple, lucid, spontaneous, occurring.

Preparing to crush the cabbage butterfly, I think of a magnolia petal come alive, & let it go.

Hove, England

Asthma

Barely two, with my red rag-dog called *Woo-Woo*, coughing up
Its expectorant name, cradling it all night, my face pink
From gasping, pink as *Woo-Woo*'s color-run belly.

Outside, father curses a sickly gene. Mother is tearful & smokes
  a Rothman's.
Dr. Garland's unshaved face is close, thick as a scrubbing brush.
His hands massage my chest.

Beyond him, wheezing rain presses to the window.
Beyond that, hospital waits, scrubbed & ready.

Everywhere the smell of camphor.
When it's rubbed on it's bitter at first, then it rises, swells
  towards my nose & eyes.

When it reaches me I swim into thin, drawn air.
I turn inside out, until you can see my shrinking lungs,
  my tightening voice & tears.

Now I'm in a place where everything's quick with panic.
Where people stare down through whorls & circles.
Rainbows swirl in my aching head,

And even my angel's short of breath.

Dusk, Scircleville

Dusk enters the coppice.
It becomes the blue-black silhouettes of maples & basswoods.
The liquid silhouettes of basswoods that exhilarate & dissolve.

Dusk presses its iron to the wide earth.
Gray-blue steam rises from the straightened, pleated fields.

Into the tilled & planed corn fields flycatchers drop
    from the sagging yarn of telephone wires.
Or are they voices, suddenly fading into grief?

Dusk opens the shambling barns & finds rusting combines
    that remember the fresh blueness of steel.
It enters the liquor store, & the Lutheran church, where
    inconsolable light floods the stoop.

Farmhouses are set adrift in these still seas,
Their lamps nodding, their sails furled,
Because hope is lost—

The hard life patiently grows quiet in the cottages

Joan

Twenty years after they stitched her & said she'd die she died.
It was spring then: leaves were sewn on branches,
    & an embroidery of stocks rose

From the looping, consuming root-work beneath the garden.
But her gift was time, & she was a genius, knitting minutes
    into rows, hours into squares of tight color.

So months were woolen blankets that cascaded from her knees,
And seasons? It was she who gave them shape & color—

The needles thick as arms when she showed me. I dropped
    stitch after stitch.
It's nothing we can learn. Supernatural, perhaps.

Like the way she mended watches, in Patcham, in the thirties.
Anyone remembers who shakes one now like a sopping rag,
    time's tight cancer coiled in the cogs,

How she'd strap them to the legs of those tenpenny hens
    in the yard—
These stories over & over. Like knitting.

Until they're caught in the easy knots of memory.
Until they're something we wear.

Her bright needles out-ticking the clock, somewhere,
    in everything I hear.
Their tiny hands coming together, minutest joy.

Late January

On the baptism of Lucy Amber Morrison

1.
Frost smell, frost light descend the hill, arm in arm
like the brother-poets Tu Fu & Li Po.
Says one to the other: "The elixir of immortality has eluded us—"

The winter eludes us.
Sparrows have already nested in the attic; amber-colored leaf-buds
like peppercorns on the maple.
Tiny hooks of queen anne's lace grappling to this life;
Milkweed sending angel seeds into the next.

The twentieth century eludes us.
It will be left to our children to make sense of it;
To dovetail image & voice into the sides of a box
in which they'll carry history.

Look behind what we know, & what we cannot know clings there,
Like frost on the underside of an oak leaf.

2.
In the crook of the maple a hooded crow works
its rusty throat-hinge.
A grocery sack flaps in the catalpa; raked leaves are heaped next
to trash cans.
Far off, a peen hammer imitates a blue jay.

Cars swoosh down South Street, swift & sure as a plane
to a panel of oak.
Quick light strokes. Then a finger tests the smoothness:

My father, guiding my hand to feel the grain.
Then my eye to the cold steel square, the spirit level.

It's how I learned of a fine sap running finger to brain.
That our senses are taproots.
That each breath's a great experiment, tenuous as slim shoots
    of narcissus,

And that failure is the complement of success, what we look for
    in art: "Who cares," wrote Lawrence, "if a poet fails?"

3.
Day has finished with its color.
Swirling dusk goes blue to black, like our jam jars when we'd
    clean brushes after art.
Teacher hanging wet paintings from a string that looped
    the classroom.

Those paintings! Clumsy imitations of reality.
Maps of the cosmos inside each of us.

Maple branches & sycamore branches dissolve, their trunks
    slim as pencils.
Now they are gone.

Light is put away with the stars.

4.
The evening sky is a vast note board; brass-colored stars pinned
    there.
On cloud-scraps are written a list of things to do,
    the dimensions of a box, *momento mori*.

A dark slick of night oozes west.
Quietly, frost lays out its precision tools; tonight, it searches for
the energy that drove the engine of summer:

Hawk moths & potter wasps are strewn like leaf springs
& cotter pins.
Burs & buttonballs, acorns & walnuts: rusted pinions, broken
bearings.

But we already know the power. It shines beyond all things
on earth. Beyond us all.
Beyond the very highest heavens.
It is that which shines in our hearts.

I know no better reason to call her Light.

Variation on “Frog Autumn” by Sylvia Plath

The sun’s wizened. A cadre of cicadas drums,
Their compadres decamped, inheriting elsewhere.
Our faces peaked, our lives shrink chitin-hard.
The skin won’t split.

Trees grow decadent. Yellow jackets loom
Like perverts at knotholes & tailpipes.
Zooming up, they snicker incomprehensible jokes.
Ears wash with screams.

In Autumn’s pale bureaucracy death’s matter-of-fact.
Crickets are strewn like pumped shells, moths
Crumble to cyanide dust. No-one speaks.
We shall never surrender.

Meccano #2 Set

assent to exquisite constraints
—Paul Valéry

As if imagination were the only impediment
And even then something empirical, to be mastered
With diligence & the right tools. The instruction manual
Was all muscular prose (*bolt this, clamp that*), the diagrams
Mockingly smug; sober-outrageous models exploded
One page, complete the next: racing cars, traction engine,
Ocean liner. No pages wasted on impatience,
Or a modeler's two fat thumbs flicking screws halfway
Across the kitchen. My father had made them all.
These the models he was building the day W.W. II broke out:
Biplanes, dreadnoughts, omnibuses—though I loved this half-
Play, half-history I loved most the detail, everything
Miniature, precision-ground: nuts that span into the arms
Of bolts, butterfly clips whose snapping into place was art.
Saturdays like this, the gas-poker in the next room
Spattering awake the fire, my brother still in bed, the big
Hoover rattling. The sun busying room to room. Hours passed.
It's easy to say memory's like Meccano, a bolting together
Not of bright tin panels but times & places. Easy, in both,
To disregard directions, substitute parts, to compromise:
The car I built only a Buggati by name, only half-built.
It had a wonky chassis, awkward bullet-shaped body;
No steering column, no wheels, no seats—is it luck
That makes your car like their car? I guess
Some are better at this stuff than others. From the start
The box-cover never gave me the right impression.
On it, kneeling triumphant over a perfect model, two
Empire-faced boys in thirties knee-length shorts, cheeks
Pink as maps. Perspective thrusts their cantilever bridge
Right through the frame. Bully for them, I thought.

Socialist Poem #3

Hove, England, 1979

It was about marbles, those clear glass spheres with twisted colored flags hung inside. Though this was the basic form, a *onesie*. We had double-sized *twosies*, & *dobbers* double that, & *king sizers* too. But aesthetics were another matter: stained glass *clearsies*, wine red, or perfect blue nuggets of sky; *oilsies*, quavering pearls of gasoline; *chinas*, porcelain tears brushed with faint ink. Our pockets bulged with wads of these glass spawn. Our book bags chimed with choirs of tiny bells.

We organized competitions in our workbooks; Math Whizz calculating ratios as to let small marbles play the big: a onesie versus a twosie was two to one against & had to hit the twosie twice to claim it. Though beauty complicated this basic math, & third parties had to be summoned: which was more coveted, an orange china dobber or a oilsie king size? What about a clear blue onesie versus a twosie with a mud-brown flag? Yet when the blunt bell spattered we'd run into playtime regardless, spilling our easy joy.

Always a count at day's end; kids with the dull shock of loss, or the gladness of a full bag, like a sack of gold doubloons. And each Monday the champion was challenged by one of those who'd bought the newest, most exotic forms: a rose-red king size china, or a new genus of scintillating oilsie. But one day a kid went too far. So wonderful. I mean his wit & cheek, sneaking into the council bus depot & stealing a huge ball-bearing, the kind used for bus wheels. It was the size of a good fist. Each of us wanted to hold it, to be left with the sweet smell of grease & steel printed on our palms.

We made it a thousand to one against a onesie. The current champ, a sea-green oilsie king-size that melted hearts the way big kids said love did, was fifty to one against. So the contender stood ten yards from the oilsie, cranked his arm back & let fly. Only it shot past the target & zipped through trees that lined the fence, blasted the fence & bounced across the road, landing a metallic punch in the passenger door of a parked Granada. *Christ.* I can still recall the silence, & the sunlight bleeding through the splintered hole; the teachers starting to run, & that high tear-brimmed voice that cracked the quiet like an egg: *you idiot, Gary, you fucking idiot . . .*

If There Must Be Faith Let It Be In Poetry

I'll pray for it. Sunday. Evening simmers; colors are drained
    & laid to one side.
Dotted light strewn on the vinca as if strained through
    a colander.
Or leaded windows.

From middle distance church bells of St. Boniface asking why
    we turned from God.
Of St. Aquinas, wondering what happened to our "natural
    orientation toward the infinite."

All around, heroic attempts to settle the old conflict,
    faith versus reason:
Kids throw a stolen sneaker high into the silver maple.

The shoe becomes a blue jay; its song
Is a nail aching from the wood.

Germinal

So soon? Maple seeds scythe April air, tracing slow catenaries,
Or else, they're suicide-leaping sky divers, until the breeze
Catches their flukes & their wing-shapes bellow; some
Alighting gentle as hen chicks hopping from a cupped hand,
Others landing with whooping crane swoops & a running
Thud, like the pilots of early pedal-cranked flight, those
Corkscrew copters, or the slapstick ice-skates-&-rocket,
Arm-wings flapping fast as the reciprocity of hope & despair.
Grasp a maple key by the knuckle-lump of its seed-husk.
Why *knuckle*? Why not *ball-joint*? After all, one can imagine them
Wings of a vegetable bat, whose body's a Cedar-of-Lebanon cone!
Held this way the blade's less likely to snap. It will
In time, because it's a pleasure to work one's nail along
The fibrous bone that arches from the seed-joint; a very
Human pleasure to whittle one into a dawn knife, an *Ur-tool*.
Examine any & you'll find trailing edges punched & nicked
Like old rail tickets, yet they still fly with bulldog determination;
Think of W.W. II Wellingtons aerated with ack-ack holes;
Of Charlie Burdett, an honest-to-goodness family legend, flying
His wood-winged Mosquito ahead of Dresden missions, drawing
Jerry fire, fear's dark seed lodged in his brain, putting its tap-
Root down. Even with a third of a wing gone they'll smoothly
Slice the air. A quarter & they'll dervish a little, more canard
Than true wing, because their design's pragmatic, not perfect:
Simplify we say, imitating Nature, calling this, oddly, *devolution* . . .
Is it not good to travel the path of close attention?!
To hold a maple seed dart-like, between thumb & forefinger
And throw it upwards. It's a stone then, dumb as that,
But then, turning felinely, calm-quick, it falls, beveling
As it goes, air currents curling around it like tiny spiroids of wood.
And it's good to contemplate the veins of a maple seed,
How they splay from the seed-hinge, top side & bottom side,
Roping together to form the leading edge; sweeping from the edge

In the shape of an elongated *S*, or the *f*-hole of a violin.
Notice their color: golden-green, purple-green at the flattest part.
Colorful as insects, they cling in butterfly-bunches in late spring
Waiting for sugar-blood to pump through thin capillaries.
Though brittle, they're muscular; strong enough to carry the weight
Of comparison; deft enough to deflect any metaphor
As they *helicopt*, as they *gyroscope* . . . Of course, they do neither!
It's just this time of year we're humbled, picking up the theory
And practice of aeronautics from our porches by the handful.

Homage to Salvatore Quasimodo

Late summer. Dusk stretches its cellophane across the sky.
The railroad crossing's stupid arms come down; the bell rattling
its silver teeth—*in me evening is falling*.

When the train evaporates, people cross into Hell, & the child
whose face is a plain bone-china plate looks up,
Her smile smeared ketchup, her father spooning out the words
like jelly:

Fuck you . . . Did you hear that? Fuck you . . .
Fuck you . . .

The Badger

Now for this poem we must remember that European badgers
(*Meles meles*) have a ferocity belying the obvious charm of
their plump hirsuteness & the cuteness of those concordant
snout-stripes, its *badge*, which is, after all, meant as warning.
That in order to dig their sets into the bone-hard chalk of the
Sussex Downs they're endowed with formidable, pneumatic
forelegs; claws like six iron grapple-hooks; & a blunt bloody
mindedness able to crush stumps.
Remember also they're night-loving, copse-dwelling, so the
suburban incandescence of Engineerium Hill, where I
straddled my bike that night, must have had the same effect
on the badger that dark's strange drug had on me.
It stared wildly; its eyes the twin hubs of that boozy night; stars
were spinning round them, the constellations of cow
parsnip. A batter drop of soda light defined a kind of no-
man's land between us.
I'd like to say the badger flinched first, its snout flared, canines
clearly bared. I'd even stage a fight; have man outwit
instinctive rage, emerging scathed yet triumphant. But that's
not how it went.
Something pulled the human in. I took one clumsy step, & the
bike clattered to the pavement. The badger bolted, vaulting a
low garden wall. Did it matter I froze moon-stiff? A privet
bush bent with its shuffling weight, its gravity.

Arthropod

1.
Cicadas are at their grindstones, each insect a source of light.
Their zillion sparks ignite the dawn.

I'm reminded of how my father sharpened his old chisels.
I'd crank the stone & he'd bend to it. His shoulders were two
huge granite rocks.

And from the chisel's blade a luminous spray, & my hand
out to catch it.
Surprising cold in the heart of light.

Like my toy gun that flashed when fired; its tiny flint, a planet,
whizzing inside.

2.
Late summer: web-laundry suspended between the hydrangea,
rose, & rhododendron.
Cocooned flies hanging from silk-strings like a collection
of chamber pots.

Cross spiders are the perfect measure of a Sunday.
In the morning, they're the color of tea dregs & toast.
By two o'clock, carpet slippers.
At dusk, a burning stub of tobacco in my father's pipe.

All evening they remain at the center of their webs: beer bubbles
rising in a tall glass.
They arch their legs in the way a child holds its fingers
when forming a house.

3.
The night was lofty, buttressed by the stone sound of crickets
& cicadas.
I found the mantis on an ATM. The time on my receipt, 8:46pm.

The mantis gleamed as if plastic. Its eyes were two black beads
from a cheap rosary.
Its long face reminded me of a priest I once knew,
Fr. Harrington.

It gave me a benediction, tut-tutting to itself, its forelimbs
praying. Not exactly . . .
Rubbing together.

Reading Oppen

Jack planes   Bradawls   Claw hammers
Iron's bone-look & bone-feel

Paintbrushes in soup cans   Mutton grease for saws
Cobwebs in the breeze-bellows breathing the way old men breathe

Cross spiders pricked out in the nebular silk

this matter-
of fact defines

poetry

• • •

Varicose fruit from the bronchial Bramley
Gourd-dry broad beans strung to a post

to see them / Is to know ourselves

The bill-hook's high crescent moon

• • •

I'm building a fence, thinking of

Clarity   Precision   Judicious cutting
Instincts shared by the wood

Set-square   edge-tool   tenon saw
The *shirt-off* rhythm of the rip saw *Carpenter, how wild the planet is*

Oak cuts dropping into apple leaves the way Oppen's fragments

Things fall   *Something balanced*   *Move*

• • •

Something from my own *Daybook*: "I'm becoming scared
of poetry."

Was I drunk?!—

There is a force of clarity... / We suffer a certain fear

• • •

Autumn sun hangs like a disk saw   The wind coughs
& clears its phlegm
Margarine light from the toolshed

Wood cat-curls as the chisel strokes through

The eternity of things astonishes a brief duration

Sycamore leaves   Snail shells   Hazelnuts awled
by squirrels
These scraps—!

Curlicues of heartwood where the drill bit's been

• • •

Dusk   Cold air pulls on its rubber band
Hover flies rout half-rotten apples   Slug tracks on the saw horse

Pillbugs   Crane flies   Earwigs the size of wood screws
A sudden breeze-lifting of hazel leaves

The snapping-to of a dovetail joint—

I have not and never did have any motive of poetry
But to achieve clarity

Beneath Our World There's Nothing but Other Worlds

A poem is a bird that migrates from the Specific to the Eternal.
This time of year the weather in the Eternal is warmer.

One bird didn't get there though, & has crashed into the lawn.
Now it's cold & real, like a stone or dead leaf.
It's one of those ordinary things we think of as simple:

Those slick feathers are as unremarkable as damp filaments
    of bluegrass;
Its broken neck is twisted in homage to branches of the red bud;
One upturned eye: a dim planet aligned with the bleakest month.

And in the hollow of its back—beneath the rib-bone pillars
    of the one true church—
Larvae are hatching from an egg-nebula, such wet & infinite stars.

Socialist Poem #4

Norwich, England, 1992

At the Bluebell Allotments on Dereham Road fifty pence could buy you a one-eighth furlong plot of clay-sand loam. For life. Fifty pence. I took one my senior year; earth so fertile I could thrust my arms in up to my shoulders; deep enough that my fork would sometimes plunge & keep going, & I'd lunge, falling over, snickering helplessly. Oh, that cold sweet eternal dirt; that paternal, encyclopedic muck where I turned up badger skulls & clay pipes, crude bricks & fossil shells, art deco pill bottles & the key to a large & simple lock.

At the gardener's co-op I bought a bag of seed-potatoes. They were a sack of dumpy souls that I lay in little graves, heaping the blessèd earth above them with a spud hoe. I also bought parsnip seeds, impossibly small, a bag of crushed laughter. I planted a jar of broad beans, every one a fixed feline eye, & broccoli that became my woolly fold of vegetable sheep. I grew courgettes, carrots, French runners, cerebral cauliflowers. Fruits, too: a stubborn bramble that extruded its berries as if precious stones, & plump, pampered strawberries hay-coddled in a ceramic tub. And, in spring, a rhubarb patch opened embryonic leaves like ragged wings that slowly swelled, stronger every day.

Kenny, my neighbor, helped me. He reminded me of those farmers in the haiku of Japanese poets; priests of a living tabernacle, with hoes instead of crosiers, &, for acolytes, riversnails, crickets, toads: *The man pulling radishes / pointed the way / with a radish*. Except it was beetroot that he'd wave at me, grasping the sprigged leaves like hair, so that the four flushed roots became the shrunken heads of state bureaucrats, or the hearts of chartered accountants, in which case the stems were still-pulsing veins.

Kenny had a thick *Nah'fohk* accent, & gout, which I didn't think you could get anymore. He spoke in archaisms: "art" for "are", the familiar "thou", &, beautiful word, "wherefore", as in "Oi wen't'th' toan 'all wherefore to collec' moi dole." He had worked at every factory in town: *Colman's, Fisons', Silver Spoon, Rountree-Nestlé*. His last job was washing bottles at the *Coca-Cola* distribution plant. After that he'd had enough, hadn't worked since. Didn't need to, because he lived off his two meticulous plots. Generous with tools, with a share of his crop, he was resistant, tough, subsistent; his relic life best suited to history books, or the stories of older folks who'd tell it like a parable.

It isn't going to last. Once, there was enough arable land in Norwich for every citizen. Now half the plots lay fallow, too choked with grass to speak. The sprawling university was getting closer, the housing estates, where daffodil backhoes & crocus-orange levelers sprouted beyond the chain-link fence. Soon there'd be launderettes, parking at convenient rates, shrink-wrapped mini-marts. Who cares? Least of all us gownies. Thursday nights, at the college Labour Club, we'd clamour to quote our Marx, Proudhon, Gramsci. Nobody dare propose the other, unglamorous, solution: Fourier, Owen, *Garden Cities*. "What a joke," we'd say, spilling our subsidized rums & coke, "reactionary socialism!" Then we'd set about saving our student grants.

Abstract

The *Encyclopedic*
History of Light,
In a footnote
To Appendix III
("More Examples
Of Coruscation"),

Shall include
Today, & how finely
Sieved sun
Sifts through paralyzed

Rain. You'll find
Cosecants &
Quadratics; cladograms &
Exploded views.
Full exposition
In the objective mode.

But what of the blown
Glass boughs
Of silver maples
Snapping-on like neon?

Or tiny bone
China lamps all
Over the catalpa?

Amber-colored
Beads that drip from
Branches of an ash.

Georgics, Tipton County

The strict lines of corn-stubble: narrow feint in which the dead
Are recorded in their own blood: *skunk, raccoon, possum—*

Farm-dogma. Plough-tactic.
Scarlet combines pillage soybeans. Bleary gray-clad hopper cars
    shuffle in their chains at the elevator.
Harrows torture the tight-lipped fields, but they don't flinch,
Though squared-off clods sun-glint, beading the pursed soil.

We're refugees in our mute cars. We blind ourselves. The sun
    too, cataracted.
Sallow clouds slough from its sunken socket, from the fallow
    sky-skin.

The stench of mildewed soy, like a sodden trench coat.
Cold air thin as the space between starved ribs. Corn-bones jag
    through chernozem.
Night closes lid, then lid—

And, yonder, a boy tills a tiny field; five quicksilver shares jitter
    behind his *Toro*.
This is how they learn.

The Gnomist

Our golden palms shaking with linseed oil.
Our thumbs doughing the whiting over & over, turning it flesh-
    soft & flesh-yellow,
Putty-smell like incense—

In a boy's imagination we were gods, molding multitudes
    from chalk & grease—

Then, pane after pane of the greenhouse was jimmied in,
    a jigsaw of light.
A celestial dome for court astronomers to gaze at in cities
    far below.
We were remote, but not vengeful.

My father, booming voice of the wilderness, haunter
    of dreams, reduced to aphorism:

"Read *The Ragged Trousered Philanthropists*," he said to me, once.
Then, five years later, "*The Way of All Flesh*."

Train Wreck with Suicide

To think what he must have thought. The train's lamp first
  distant star, then moon, then looming all at once.
But that is too much, a stretch.

At first they can't even find a body, the car crushed to a puzzle,
  cops all over it,
Hazard lamps urging them on & on & on.

Then someone points into the wreck.
Others peer & nod as if they've seem something trivial, a dead cat.
More arrivals: an ambulance lurches up the hill, a tow truck, a cub
  reporter, thankful for this story.

What work's done is done alone. Bearable this way, efficient.
Even our crowd, off to one side, seems necessary.
A young cop eyes us, saying nothing, though I rehearse my answer,
  a nonchalant *oh, I live here*,
But I'm lost as to why I stay.

For an hour. Quick really, so much to think of: crushed glass
  like sherbet; half-mile of cars (fresh-minted trucks, by-products
  of corn) going north.
Crossing bells still ringing: great, I think, *death-knell*;
Until the Norfolk Southern truck, the gate arms lifting in relief.

Necks crane when a gurney's lifted down. But there's nothing,
  a shape wrapped & strapped,

Then slid into the ambulance, the wheeled legs snapping back
  into place as a cricket's do, taking flight.

This done & the tow-truck hauls away the wreck.
The train's dragged off by another, & our crowd dissolves into

ritual: a dog is walked, used cars revved in the lot,
Lamps coming on behind curtains.

Something of this turning away is grief, I hope, because we
suffer of the dead only scattered things:
Windshield glass in bunches, grape-green, broken rail ties, sheet
steel twisted into leaf-shapes,

And trapped in the branches of the railroad a livid moon,
And, from the corn refinery, the sweet-sick smell of syrup.

Winter Storm, Mid-December

after George Oppen "Route"

After, there's always clarity, the weather, as they say, *lifting*.
Street lamps come on, firing their flash bulbs. The moon's eye
dilates.
From another garden, a child's laughter.

A cat lifts her body clear of snow, & a tree loses a branch
like an eyelash.
The sound of plows a block over on Columbia. One by one
these too dissolve.
Now there's just snow, blue as the skin of an egg:
surely clarity is the most beautiful thing in the world,
A limited, limiting clarity

Yes, so I thought, putting the pan of water on my bedroom sill
that time.
Twenty degrees outside, &, slowly, precise, I watched the noon-
light swell into a disc of ice,
My breath pulsed on the leaded pane—limited, limiting.

Notes to the Poems

"November, the Wabash River":
The final line is from Tomas Tranströmer "Sketch in October." Trans. Robin Fulton. *Selected Poems 1954-1986*. Ed. Robert Hass. Hopewell: Ecco, 1987.

"Dusk, Scircleville":
The final line is from Georg Trakl "Evening Muse." Trans. Lucia Getsi. *Poems*. Athens: Mundus Artium Press, 1973.

"Late January":
Tu Fu and Li Po: Chinese poets of the T'ang period, c. 8th Century AD. Quotation is from Tu Fu's poem "For Li Po." Trans. David Hinton. *The Selected Poems of Tu Fu*. New York : New Directions, 1989.

D.H. Lawrence quotation is from "Chaos in Poetry" in *Phoenix: The Posthumous Papers* of D.H. Lawrence. Ed. V. de Sola Pinto and F.W. Roberts. New York: Viking, 1936.

The fourth section contains an allusion to the Hindu "Chandogya Upanishad" in *The Upanishads*. Trans. Juan Mascaró. Harmondsworth: Penguin, 1987.

"Homage to Salvatore Quasimodo":
The quotation in line 2 is from "Sunken Oboe." Trans. Jack Bevan. *Salvatore Quasimodo: Complete Poems*. New York: Schocken, 1984.

"Reading Oppen":
Italicized lines are George Oppen's. They are taken from the *Collected Poems of George Oppen* (New York: New Directions, 1976) and from the "Daybook" (first published in *Iowa Review 88*).

"Socialist Poem #4":

The haiku in the third stanza is by Issa and is taken from Robert Hass's essay "Images" in *Twentieth Century Pleasures*. New York: Ecco, 1984.

The "Socialist Poems" were inspired by Campbell McGrath's series the "Capitalist Poems."

Photo by Fuzzy Gerdes

Martin Walls was born in Brighton, and grew up in the sister town of Hove in Southern England. His poems have appeared in *Boulevard*, *The Nation*, *The Gettysburg Review*, *Five Points*, *Passages North*, and elsewhere. He graduated with a baccalaureate in American Literature from the University of East Anglia, Norwich in 1993, and with an MFA from Purdue University in 1997. In 1998 he was awarded the Discovery/ *The Nation* Joan Leiman Jacobsen Poetry Prize. He has taught poetry at Ball State University and Purdue University, and currently lives in Solvay, New York with his wife, Christine.

New Issues Press Poetry Series

James Armstrong, *Monument in a Summer Hat*
Anthony Butts, *Fifth Season*
Gladys Cardiff, *A Bare Unpainted Table*
Lisa Fishman, *The Deep Heart's Core Is a Suitcase*
Edward Haworth Hoeppner, *Rain Through High Windows*
Josie Kearns, *New Numbers*
Lance Larsen, *Erasable Walls*
David Dodd Lee, *Downsides of Fish Culture*
Deanne Lundin, *The Ginseng Hunter's Notebook*
Joy Manesiotis, *They Sing to Her Bones*
David Marlatt, *A Hog Slaughtering Woman*
Paula McLain, *Less of Her*
Malena Mörling, *Ocean Avenue*
Julie Moulds, *The Woman With a Cubed Head*
Marsha de la O, *Black Hope*
C. Mikal Oness, *Water Becomes Bone*
Margaret Rabb, *Granite Dives*
Rebecca Reynolds, *Daughter of the Hangnail*
John Rybicki, *Traveling at High Speeds*
Diane Seuss-Brakeman, *It Blows You Hollow*
Marc Sheehan, *Greatest Hits*
Angela Sorby, *Distance Learning*
Russell Thorburn, *Approximate Desire*
Martin Walls, *Small Human Detail in Care of National Trust*
Patricia Jabbeh Wesley, *Before the Palm Could Bloom: Poems of Africa*